WHAT ON EARTH IS A
BOOBY ?

JENNY TESAR

A BLACKBIRCH PRESS BOOK
WOODBRIDGE, CONNECTICUT

Published by Blackbirch Press, Inc.
One Bradley Road, Suite 104
Woodbridge, CT 06525

Printed in Hong Kong

10 9 8 7 6 5 4 3 2 1

Photo Credits

Cover and title page: ©Patti Murray/Animals Animals.
Pages 4—5: ©Tim Davis/Photo Researchers, Inc.; pages 6—7: ©Stan Osolinski/Animals
Animals; page 8: ©Gerard Lacz/Animals Animals; page 9 (top): ©Gilbert S. Grant/Photo
Researchers, Inc; page 9 (below left): ©B.G. Murray, Jr./Animals Animals; page 9 (below
right): ©David C. Fritts/Animals Animals; pages 10—11: ©Mickey Gibson/Animals Animals;
page 13: ©G.L. Kooyman/Animals Animals; pages 14—15: ©Joe McDonald/Animals Animals;
page17: ©Frans Lanting/Photo Researchers, Inc.; page18: ©G.L. Kooman/Animals Animals;
page 19: ©Joe McDonald/Animals Animals; page 20: ©Mickey Gibson/Animals Animals;
page 20—21: ©Warwick Johnson/Animals Animals; pages 20—23 ©David C. Fritts/Animals
Animals; page 23: ©Patti Murray/Animals Animals; page 24: ©Carl Purcell/Photo
Researchers, Inc.; page 25: ©David C. Fritts/Animals Animals; page 26: ©Patti Murray/
Animals Animals; page 27: ©Gilbert S. Grant/ Photo Researchers, Inc.; page 29: ©B.G./
Animals Animals.

Library of Congress Cataloging-in-Publication Data
Tesar, Jenny E.
What on earth is a booby? / Jenny Tesar. — 1st ed.
    p.   cm. — (What on earth series)
    Includes bibliographical references (p.   ) and index.
    ISBN 1-56711-094-0 : $12.95
    1. Boobies (Birds)—Juvenile literature.   [1. Boobies (Birds)
2. Birds.]   I. Title.   II. Series.
QL696.P48T47   1994
598.4'3—dc20
                                                                94-27856
                                                                        CIP
                                                                        AC

What does it look like?

Where does it live?

What does it eat?

How does it reproduce?

How does it survive?

TURN THESE PAGES AND FIND OUT!

A MASKED BOOBY WATCHES OVER ITS NEST HIGH ABOVE THE WATER IN ECUADOR.

A booby is a bird that lives near the sea. It is about the size of a goose. Boobies live in groups called colonies. A colony may contain thousands of boobies.

Boobies have webs between the toes of their feet. The webs help them swim in the sea. Some boobies have very bright and colorful feet. There are blue-footed boobies and red-footed boobies.

The name *booby* comes from the Spanish word *bobo*. It means "stupid fellow." Hungry sailors gave the birds this name because boobies are very easy to catch. The birds cannot seem to learn that people can be their enemies.

A BLUE-FOOTED BOOBY SPREADS ITS LONG WINGS. LIKE ALL BIRDS, BOOBIES HAVE WINGS AND BODIES COVERED WITH FEATHERS.

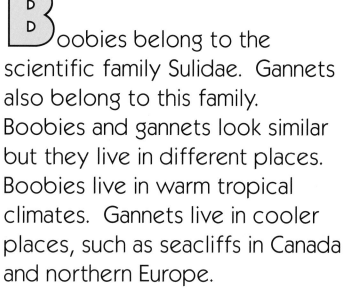

Boobies belong to the scientific family Sulidae. Gannets also belong to this family. Boobies and gannets look similar but they live in different places. Boobies live in warm tropical climates. Gannets live in cooler places, such as seacliffs in Canada and northern Europe.

Like all birds, boobies and gannets have a pair of wings. Their bodies are covered with feathers. Feathers help a bird to fly. They also keep a bird warm.

Boobies and gannets have long wings and a long tail. They have short legs and webbed feet. Their bills are long and pointed.

A RED-FOOTED BOOBY.

There are six kinds, or species, of boobies. In English, these species are called the blue-footed booby, red-footed booby, masked booby, brown booby, Peruvian booby, and Abbott's booby. They have different names in other languages.

Each species has its own scientific name. This name is the same in every language, all over the

LEFT: A BROWN BOOBY.
BELOW RIGHT: A BLUE-
FOOTED BOOBY. BELOW
LEFT: A MASKED BOOBY.

9

What On Earth
Is a Booby?

world. A scientific name has two parts. The first part is the genus. All boobies and gannets belong to the genus *Sula*. This is an ancient Icelandic name for the Northern gannet.

The second half of the name says something about the species. For example, the brown booby's scientific name is *Sula leucogaster*. *Leucogaster* means "white belly." The belly of some brown boobies is covered with beautiful white feathers.

The body of a booby is designed to move easily through air and water. It is shaped like a torpedo. The wings are long and pointed. The tail is long and narrow.

Under a booby's skin are sacs that are filled with air. These sacs protect the bird when it dives head-first into water—just like an air bag in a

A BOOBY'S BODY IS SHAPED LIKE A TORPEDO. IT IS DESIGNED TO MOVE QUICKLY THROUGH THE AIR AND WATER.

car protects a human in a crash. These features help the booby survive in an ocean environment.

Male and female boobies look similar, but the females weigh more than the males and make different sounds. When two friendly brown boobies meet, the male whistles. The female honks or grunts.

Boobies live in tropical places. They are found in warm parts of the Atlantic, Pacific, and Indian oceans. They spend the day flying over the ocean surface, looking for food in the water below. As darkness comes, they return to land. Most boobies spend the night on the ground. But red-footed and Abbott's boobies sit on trees.

Boobies are strong flyers. They are also very powerful divers. Out of water, they waddle. Their legs are short, which makes them clumsy on land.

OPPOSITE: A RED-FOOTED BOOBY SITS IN ITS NEST ABOVE THE GROUND.

A GROUP OF BLUE-
FOOTED BOOBIES
SWARMS OVER THE
OCEAN IN SEARCH
OF FISH.

Flying and all the other activities of life require energy. Boobies get energy from the food they eat. Their main food is fish. They eat many kinds of fish, including mullet, anchovies, sea catfish, and flying fish.

As a booby flies over the water, it watches below for signs of fish. When it sees a fish, it dives down at great speed. It grabs and holds the fish with its long, pointed bill. Then the booby swallows the fish whole.

Most boobies live on islands. They share the islands with many other living things. For example, several kinds of boobies live on the Galápagos Islands off the coast of South America. Other birds live there too, including penguins, owls, hawks, pelicans, and gulls. Giant turtles and large lizards crawl over rocks. Crabs creep along the water's edge.

North America

Atlantic Ocean

Central America

Galápagos
Islands

South America

Pacific Ocean

**COMMON TERRITORY
OF THE BOOBY**

OPPOSITE: A RED-FOOTED BOOBY WATCHES AS A PAIR OF TERNS VISITS
THE BOOBY'S TERRITORY.

Frigatebirds live on the same islands as boobies. They are enemies of boobies. These birds are named after a kind of ship called a frigate. Pirates often used frigates. The frigatebird is a kind of pirate of the air.

When a frigatebird sees a booby carrying a fish, it chases the booby. It pesters the booby until the booby drops the fish. The frigatebird then grabs the fish in mid-air and gulps it down.

OPPOSITE: THE GREAT FRIGATEBIRD IS AN ENEMY OF THE BOOBY.

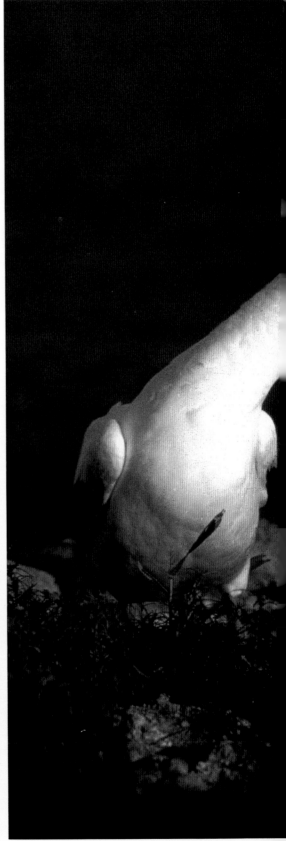

Each pair of boobies has its own territory, or piece of land, in a colony. This territory is where they build their nest and raise their young. Boobies will protect their territory against other boobies. If another booby comes too close, they will peck at it.

A PAIR OF MASKED BOOBIES GUARDS ITS TERRITORY.

TWO MALE BOOBIES CLASH AT A NESTING SITE.

TWO BLUE-FOOTED BOOBIES
COURTING ON A BEACH.
RIGHT: A MALE BLUE-FOOTED BOOBY
LIFTS HIS HEAD AND FLAPS HIS WINGS
IN A COURTSHIP DISPLAY.

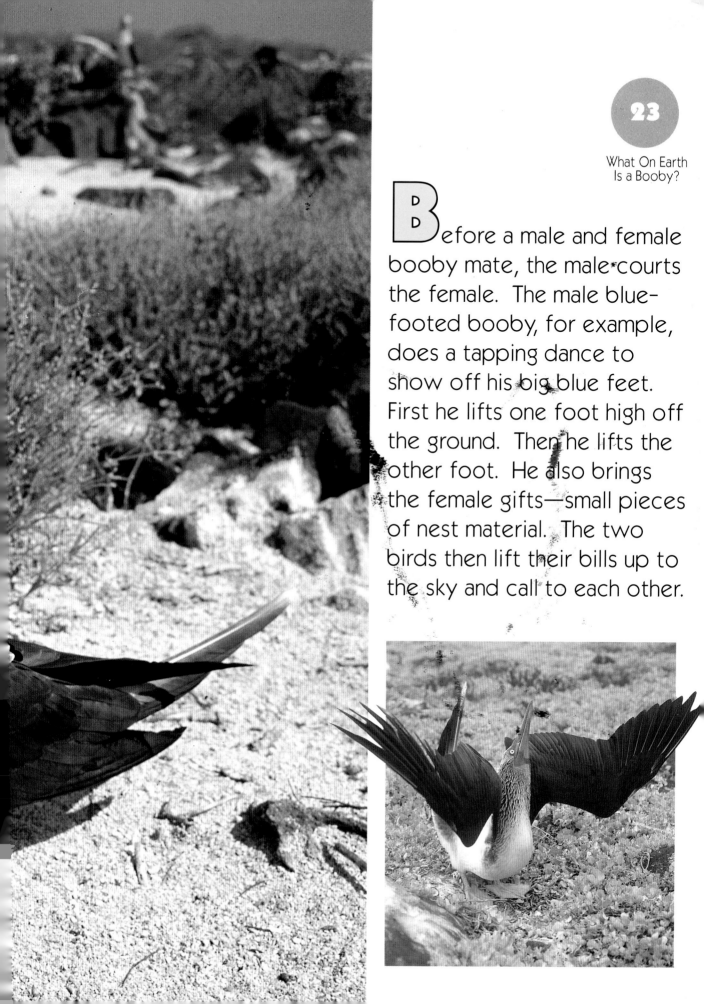

Before a male and female
booby mate, the male courts
the female. The male blue-
footed booby, for example,
does a tapping dance to
show off his big blue feet.
First he lifts one foot high off
the ground. Then he lifts the
other foot. He also brings
the female gifts—small pieces
of nest material. The two
birds then lift their bills up to
the sky and call to each other.

A MALE AND FEMALE BOOBY MATING.

Mating is part of reproduction, which is one of life's most important processes. Reproduction means "making more of the same." When boobies reproduce, they create new boobies. Without reproduction, boobies would no longer exist. They would become extinct.

During mating, sex cells called sperm pass from the male into the female. The sperm join with, or fertilize, egg cells in the female. Each fertilized egg is covered with a shell before it is laid.

Eggs must be kept warm if they are to develop into baby birds. The male and female boobies take turns keeping their eggs warm under their big, webbed feet.

A BOOBY PARENT WARMS ITS EGGS AS IT GUARDS ITS NEST.

A BOOBY CHICK, ONLY A FEW WEEKS OLD, BEGS FOR FOOD FROM ITS MOTHER.

A NEWBORN BOOBY IN ITS NEST SHORTLY AFTER HATCHING.

At birth, a baby booby is about the size of a mouse. It cannot see and is almost naked. Its eyes open when it is a few days old. Soon it is covered with soft feathers.

Baby boobies grow quickly. When they are about two months old, they are as big as their parents. By the time they are three to five months old, they are able to fly.

Until a baby booby is able to fly and catch its own food, its parents take very good care of it. They keep it warm and protect it from enemies. Each day, they bring it food to eat.

Because of human activities, many booby colonies have disappeared. People have hunted boobies for food. They have also collected and eaten the eggs of boobies. Construction and mining have destroyed the nesting grounds of many boobies around the world.

Humans compete with boobies at sea, too. Fishing fleets catch anchovies and other fish that are an important part of the booby's diet. With less food available, many of the birds starve.

Some of the remaining booby colonies are now protected by laws that do not allow hunting. Colonies such as those in the Galápagos Islands are protected because they are in national parks.

Boobies are beautiful and fascinating creatures. By protecting these colorful birds, we help make sure that they will continue to be a part of the Earth's wonderful, rich environment.

OPPOSITE: A COLONY OF PERUVIAN BOOBIES GATHERS ON THE STEEP ROCKS OF COASTAL PERU.

Glossary

air sacs Spaces under a booby's skin that are filled with air.

colony A group of animals that live together.

environment Surroundings. A booby's environment includes everything around it: rocks, plants, air, water, and many kinds of animals.

extinct No longer in existence. Dinosaurs are examples of extinct animals.

fertilization The joining of a male sex cell, called a sperm, and a female sex cell, called an egg. Fertilization is a part of reproduction.

reproduction Making more creatures of the same kind.

scientific name A name for a species that is the same everywhere in the world. It has two parts. For example, the scientific name for the Abbott's booby is *Sula abbotti.*

species A group of living things that are closely related to one another. Members of a species can reproduce with one another.

territory An area that "belongs" to a certain animal or group of animals.

Further Reading

Beaty, Dave. *Waterfowl*. Plymouth, MN: Childs
World, 1993.

Brown, Mary B. *Wings Along the Waterway*. New
York: Orchard Books, 1992.

Ganeri, Anita. *Birds*. New York: Watts, 1992.

Kerrod, Robin. *Birds: Water Birds*. New York: Facts
On File, 1989.

Losito, Linda. *Birds: Aerial Hunters*. New York,
Facts On File, 1989.

Mabie, Grace. *A Picturebook of Water Birds*.
Mahwah, NJ: Troll, 1992.

Ricciuti, Edward R. *Birds*. Woodbridge, CT:
Blackbirch Press, 1993.

Root, Phyllis and McCormick, Maxine. *Galapagos
Islands*. New York: Crestwood House, 1989.

Stewart, Frances T. and Charles P. *Birds and Their
Environments*. New York: HarperCollins, 1988.

Index